deMocKracy

deMockracy

Mike Maggio

Plain View Press
P. O. 42255
Austin, TX 78704

plainviewpress.net
sb@plainviewpress.net
1-512-441-2452

Copyright Mike Maggio, 2007. All rights reserved.
ISBN: 978-1-891386-77-0
Library of Congress Number: 2007921912

Photos by Mike Maggio.

Cover by Nancy Simons from a photo by Mike Maggio.

Funding for this work has been provided by the Puffin Foundation.

$n G$d W$ Tr$st

Contents

January 18, 2003, the People	11
amerika the grate	15
Notice I	17
(obscured)	22
Notice II	26
The Guest List	27
(obscured)	29
Bizarre youzhwul	31
Alienation Blues	33
My Job	38
Sacrafishylamb	41
Shoptalk	43
Notice III	44
Flag Burning	45
oanly in am-erica	48
Hitler Is Not Dead	50
(obscured)	52
Weather Report	55
Collateral Damage	57
War of the Month Club	61
Two Soldiers	64
You Really Don't Love	65
(obscured)	66
Raw Footage	67
After the Beheading	71
We of Greenwich Village Cafe Days	73
Paper Cranes (for Anthony)	76
About the Author	79

This book has been sealed for your protection

10° F. – Protestor, January 18, 2003, Washington D.C.

Dedication

This book is dedicated to George W. Bush, President-Select of the Younited States of Am-erica, aka George II, defender of freedumb, sire of pat-riot-ism, perpetrator of lief as nvr b4 scene.

This book is dedicated to George II's duplicitous administration, to his illegal attacks on the United Nations, Europe, the people of Iraq, the Constitution, the Bill of Rights, the Civil Rights Movement, Equal Opportunity, the Environment and the basic right of people to exist in peace all around the world.

This book is dedicated to the most dangerous administration in the his-story of the cuntry.

This book is dedicated to Donald Rumsfeld, Generalissimo Emeritus and architect of the war on the world. May he never rest in peace.

This book is dedicated to John Ashrcroft, cymbal of freedumb and exemplar supreme of holier-than-thou just-ice.

This book is dedicated to Dick Cheney, Vice-President-in-Abstentia and oil-man on-high, dedicated perpetrator of secretly skewed energy policies.

This book is dedicated to Colin Powell, white man in disguise, whose devotion to world peace is exemplified by two wars waged in the very same place.

This book is dedicated to Condoleezza Rice, honorary white man and oil-vessel namesake, committed to all that is good and pure in WHITEwashing the truth.

This book is dedicated to Tom Ridge, whose presence, determination and unflinching facial expressions have made my home more less secure from bugs and warrants.

Lastly, this book is dedicated to Osama Bin Laden, self-unproclaimed prophet and honorary terrorist who, with previous training and assistance from the CIA, made all of this possible.

Bushit to the people!

Acknowledgements

Grateful acknowledgement is extended to the editors of *The L.A. Weekly, Vol. No. 1 Magazine, Synaesthetic, www.spokenwar.com, Critical Perspectives on Accounting Journal, Blue Collar Review, Beltway, Prophetic Voices* and *D.C. Poets Against the War* who were not afraid to print many of these poems.

Conquer the world with culture.

January 18, 2003, the People

The people

came
by bus, on foot
they showed up by train
they hiked the long walk from Iowa
they commuted in the crowded cars of the DC metro
they flew in by plane
they arrived from Minnesota, Wisconsin, and Oregon
they came from Maine and Vermont
from New York and Ohio
from every corner
they converged on the center of this mighty, mighty land
they came
to speak, to listen
to chant, to shout

      united

we, the people,
came
in the cold of January
200,000 strong and still coming
on this day, the day of the birth of our hero the King
in the winter of a nation whose furnaces crave to be fed
whose furnaces burnish the rich and powerful
while those in the street are forced to rub their toes for warmth
(and the people shouted "No Blood For Oil")
(and the banners pleaded "Money For Jobs Not War")

we stood in the cold
united
some
naked
some numb

some banging on drums and tympanis
together
young and old
we warmed ourselves on ideals and slogans
we warmed ourselves up
to oppose the bald arrogant orders
to reject a war of massive aggression
to expose their weapons of mass deception
and unmask their empty war heads
(and the people shouted "Blessed Are The Peace Makers")

because
united
we, the people

            will never be

beaten again
we, the people
will never be
hamstrung and trodden
again
because
we, the people
who voted for a winner
were crowned the ultimate losers
because
we, the people
having been kidnapped by demockracy
were drawn and quartered
by the marketing kings
    the TV tyrants
    the precinct persecutors
by the
       kallous kourtroom kangaroos

we who had our chads ripped out
we whose tongues have been dissected
whose voices shackled
in the name of demockracy
in this demockracy of all demockracies
we came
to speak

                                      defeated

in the name of america
we come
united
we, the people
from all over this great land
to pledge allegiance
to the nation for which we stand
licked by cold and bluster
we shout
and we will shout
and the world will shout
for liberty and justice for all

(and the voices in the street sang
the people   united   will never be   defeated

the people   united   will never be   defeated)

we   the people   will never be   defeated
we
      the people
                will never again
                                  be defeated

Anti-War Protestors, January 18, 2003, Washington D.C.

amerika the grate

pat
    riot
        ism
amerika the grate

stand tall
     stand tall
o bestial whore
let freedumb wring frm yr turrets
let libertea Trump-et a gelded song

o aMercka™
o ay be em™
o gee eeeeeeh™
o pfarm-a-suit-a-kill that U r
o U hoo taut us 2b deadphast in hour de sires
o U hoo wrought us pleazure

I am yr sect slave
bar   k
nd eye shall grovel
cum   mand
nd ay shall
o
    bey
stand e-rec   t
nd I shall reach fr uran   US
I shall mount u like a whorse
nd ride u till th goldn gait

o amercka
o dough jones
ay loooooooooooong
phor yr Midass tuch
take me trance form

inv aid my privates
that i may bow down 'n begg phor moor
ay will willkommen U into mein arms
like a jilted lvr
if oanly yr will bemine

o amerika
o amercka
ay am Erica

o li berate me o temptress st   rong
o lure me in2 th nex'um of yr malestrom
o phree me phrom the objekshun of m'I tru dezIre
o bait me o b eat me
o g odd o jes US
o title ate me o phck me good

Notice I

We fully believe
in our

(White)

people.

O sama

O sama
hosanna in high mountains
we worship your beard
we worship the ground
your holiness destroys

O sama
we thank you
for your teachings
we thank you
for showing us
a new meaning
for civil
      aviation
we thank you
for redefining
911

O sama
we laud you
for your gift
of self-righteous jihadists
we rejoice
in your mission of destroying history
for your humane and unparalleled treatment of women
(our mothers, our wives, our daughters)
we applaud you
for giving us
suicide bombers
for harboring
dirty bombs
for showing us the means to
mass destruction
self obliteration
and other acts

our vocabulary
has yet to define

O sama
you who have shirked evil
you who have embraced all that is good
you who stand proudly in your lofty humility
we praise you
for leading us not into temptation
but delivering us into annihilation
amen

without you
we could not attain heaven
without you
the people would rejoice in their depravity
without you
we would stumble to our freedom
and fester in the pestilence
we call democracy

O O sama
America loves you
because of you
we are now more secure
because of you
we are stronger
because of you
our people have united
because of you
our passion for freedom
has been curtailed
and we now bask
in the warm, vibrant glow of homeland security

O O sama

O hosanna
you are our messiah
you are a golden bird in a withered bush
you are a starved politician's very best friend
you are a gift horse with no apparent mouth

O sama
O hosanna
born in the land of prophets
warrior, chosen and nurtured by the CIA
terrorist supreme
made and patented in the USA.

Lessons from the *Bible* — The Christian(s) Left.

400 Sirens

400 sirens
    the house is on fire
    the trees are on fire
400 sirens
    screaming
    screeching
    flashing through the
    streets are on fire
400 sirens
    the men in red trucks
    the men in white coats
    the men in blue
400 sirens
    the men in helicopters
    the men in red hats
    the black man in white light
    the white men in blue coats
    the glaring red and blue
    the fading black and white
400 sirens
    screaming victim
    screaming savior
    Jerry Falwell's army
    Fahrenheit 451
    the 11 o'clock news
    11:30 bulletin
    11:59
400 sirens
    from the school
    from the shelter
    from the TV

      from the airport
      from the ships
      from the Pentagon
400 sirens
      the city's on fire
      the sky's on fire
      Centigrade 451
      Absolute 0
      nuclear freeze
      nuclear winter
400 sirens
      in my head
      revolving around my
      shivering head
400 sirens
      coming to
      save me
400 sirens
      coming to
      please save me from
400 sirens
      Jesus Christ
      save me!

WHAT'S WRONG WITH

Find the Weapons of Mass Destruction on these pages. Report your findings to your

CHEMICAL WEAPONS

BIOLOGICAL WEAPONS

NUCLEAR WEAPONS

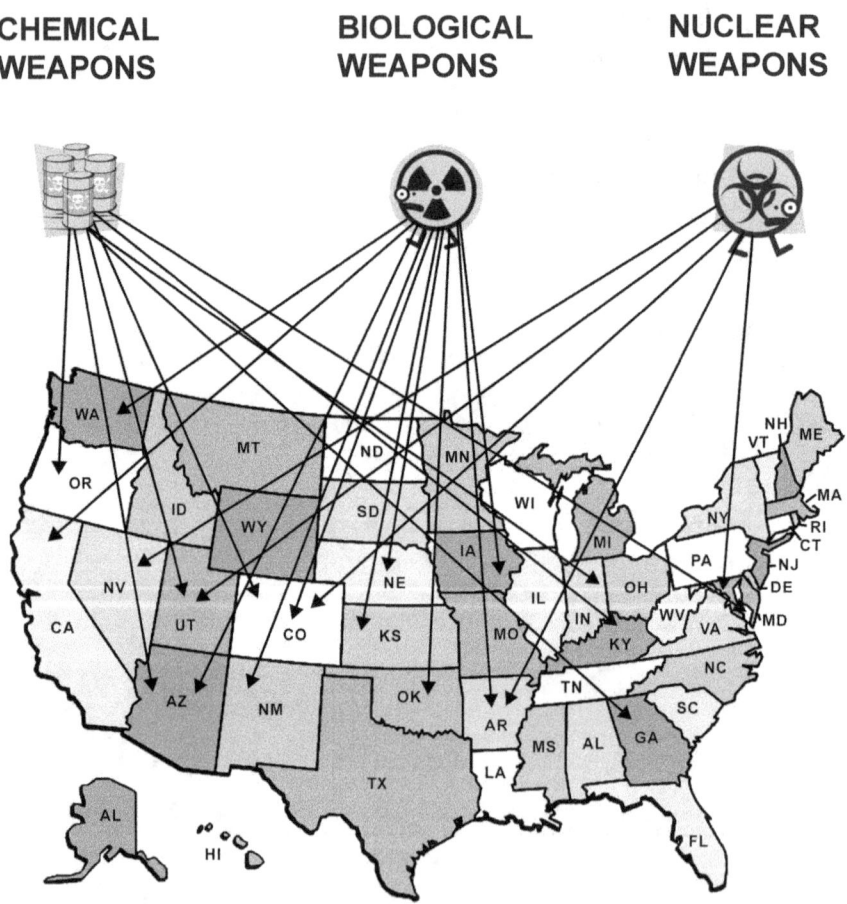

THIS PICTURE?

Use the legend as a guide.
nearest United Nations Weapons Inspector.

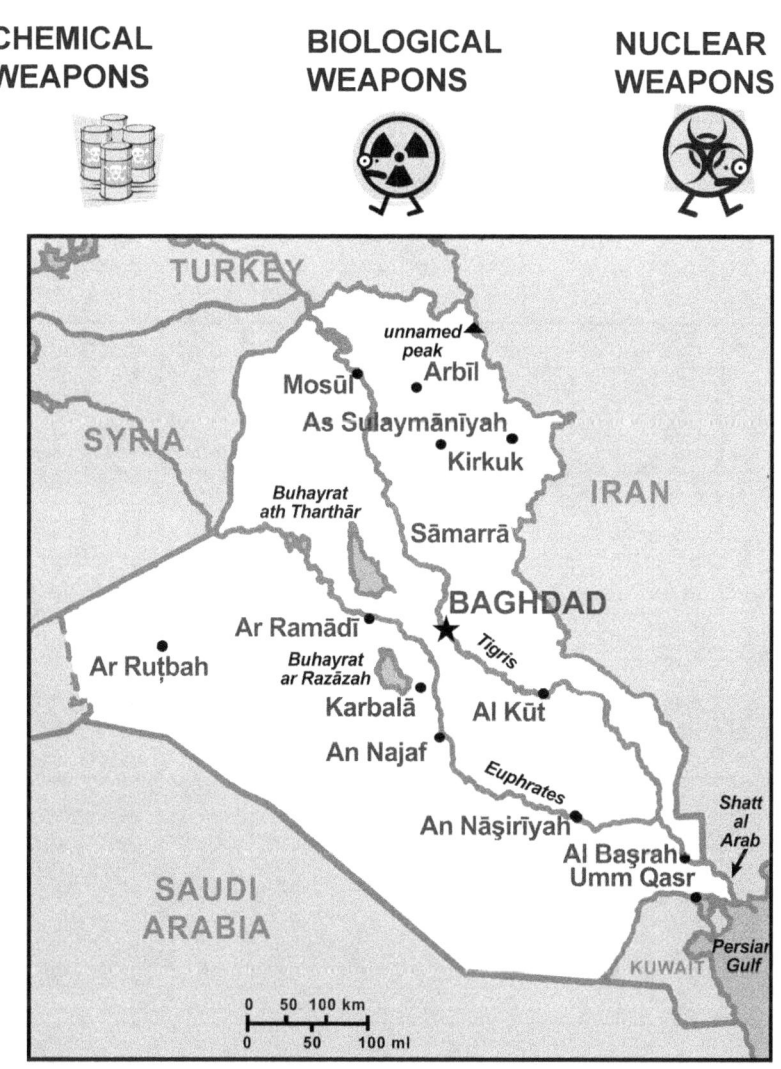

Notice II

We are
an equal opportunity

(Male)

employer.

The Guest List

Life was a series of reeling anesthetics
(sex, drugs, alcohol, television)
so one morning
when he finally woke up dead
he threw a BIG PARTY
invited all his friends
        his enemies
the women who had cunningly abused him
the men in their slinking fedoras
the yuppie in the next door condo conversion
the manager   of the local football team
                of the local fast food franchise
the President   of the United States and his lovely wife
                      (he just could not say NO to HER)
                of the National Rifle Association
                of Paine-Webber
                of United Technologies
                of CitiCorp
                of IBM
                of ABC Entertainment
the PUBLISHER of The New York Times
                  The Wall Street Journal
                  Fortune 500
                  Jane's Defense Weekly
The Commander-in-Chief of NATO
                  the Warsaw Pact
                  the Freedom Fighters of Nicaragua
                                  Angola
                                  the Cuban
                                          Resistance
                                  the Israeli
                                          Defense Forces
                      and all those who had gone out of their way
                          to kill so generously in the name of

DEMOCRACY
the heads of the CIA
        the FBI
      INTERPOL
Oliver North,   for his HEROIC act of cowardice
Donald Trump,   for his invaluable contribution to the laws of
    poverty
Henry Kissinger, for his brazen insights into the forces of evil
Dan Rather, whom he would rather have forgotten but invited
    deceitfully
                                    JUST THE SAME
George Lucas,   for his lucid blueprint for national security
George Will
Anita Bryant
Imelda Marcos
(her husband was too sick to attend)
Manuel Antonio "Pineapple" Noriega
and all the countless others
who had magnanimously supplied him
with his daily survival kit.

Of course
he would have really gone all out
had they not allowed him

TO AWAKEN AT ALL.

Quiz

(with the use of poetic license as its modus metaphorus)

Match a word in Column 1 with a word in Column 2 that is closest in meaning. Use missiles to show you choices. Score yourself on the number of answers you invent.

Patriot	Propaganda
Freedom Fighter	Jihad
Contra	Traitor
Weapons of Mass Destruction	Guerilla
Liberation	Terrorist
POW	Holy Warrior
Law & Order	Smart Bombs
War on Terror	Enemy Combatant
Military Victory	Political Capital
Embedded Reporter	Military Spokesman
News	Occupation
Criminal	Sandinista

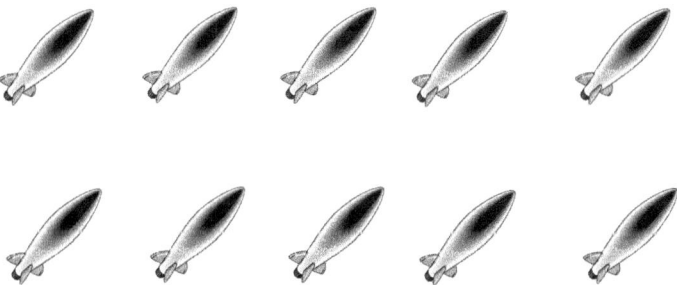

The business is giving me the business.

Biznes az youzhwul

t
   ax
       cut.
pay
      cut
the
       inevita
           bull
               Lay
                     off
              sell
                   off
     corp
         O-rate
               merger
a
     plaus
        on
             wall
                  st
                  a
            pall
        on
     main
st
home
     land
        securi
            tea
              home
        less
    in
security
stock

```
            options
stock
            phrases
in
                    flay
                        tion
            de
                        flation
the
            e
                    con
                        o
                            me
inside
            trade
                    r
law
            full
                    trait
                        or
bull
            market
            bull
shit
biznes
            az
                    you
                        zhwul
gone
            fishing
```

Alienation Blues

You invite me
with your sweet talk
with your talk talk talk
you invite me
you say
      hey Jose
my name is John
but that doesn't seem to matter
and you say
      hey Jose
  mi casa es su casa
and you tell me
      with your television eyes
      with your magazine tongue
you proclaim
      with your corporation arms
      with your military eyes
you insist
      with your rockets like penises
      with your PR like spanish flies
you say
      I   love   you
just like that
      I   love   you
      I   love   you
and you march march
      through the room
      through the house
saying
      I   love   you
shouting
      I   love   you
marching
      through the town
      through the world

screaming
  I love you
despite the fact that I'm
  too old
   and too poor
   and too ugly
and you say
  I love you
and I believe it!

Well I know what you want
it's in every statement you make
it's in your face
it's in your clothes
it's in the way you comb your hair
but I'm in such need
you seem to have what I need
I need you so bad
so I go with you
and I let you fuck me
I let you fuck me
over and over
and you fulfill my need
you fuck me over
and you fulfill my need.

Something is not right here
something is wrong
I feel like a hostage
I feel like an abortion in progress
I feel like a piece of celluloid
splitting on the screen
something is wrong here
something is definitely not right.

Well I came home today
and I saw you

I saw you
I was looking through the window
I was peeking through the door
I saw you
you were cheating on me
you were fucking with the TV
putting that goddamn box
between you and me
I wanted to smash it
I wanted to unplug that energy sucker
I wanted to murder that impostor
and you looked at me
with those eyes
with those teleprompter eyes
gloating like a drum of toxic waste on the hillside
fuming like a factory in the city
threatening me like an oil slick on the beach
and you said go ahead make my day
go ahead you said make my day
you said make my day
so I left
I ran out with my chains
I smashed a few windows
I set the house on fire
I wrote fuck you all over town

Why are you doing this to me
why are you doing this
haven't I given you what you wanted
haven't I given you everything you wanted
well I feel so bad
I feel so bad
I feel so blue
well I got the blues
yeah I got those alienation blues

it's in my lungs
it's in my corpuscles
I got them blues in my sputum
I'm blue man
well my name is Jose
but you can call me John
you can call me John
yeah you can call me John
well you can call me alienated
you can say I'm alienated
you can call me blue
yeah I got the blues
and I live in Justicetown
yeah I live in Justicetown
ain't got no bed
you've thrown me out
ain't got no home
you've thrown me out
ain't got no shelter
you've thrown me out
I sleep on the street
I sleep on the bench
I sleep in the doorway
I fuck newspapers
yeah I fuck newspapers that say
I   love   you
yeah I live in Justicetown
and I eat our of trashcans in
Justicetown
I donate blood to
Justicetown
I donate plasma to
Justicetown
ain't got no car
ain't got no money
ain't got no shoes

all I gots the blues
in Justicetown
well something is wrong in--

Alienation

                                                                         Alienation
                    Alien
                          Nation.

My Job

my job went a-walkin' up wall street
my job came a-crawlin' back down
my job spit me in a fearsome eye
my job say whatcha gonna do when we send you home
my job sing whatcha gonna say

oh yeah
       oh yeah

my job works double-ass for single-ass pay
my job is to get off welfare
my job is to stay employed
my job is to get laid off
my job is to beg for my doo-dah rights
my job is dead
my job
my job

doo
                                                                                       wah
                    doo
                          wah

my job went a-wishin' an' a-washin'
my job returned empty-handed
my job went up the river and never came back
oh my my my my

my job

my job to spend when the man say
my job to save when the man say
my job to get into doo dah debt
my job to pay it all off
my job to make the e con o me o my

it's all on me
                         on me
                                     on my job

now let me tell you something

my job is not to feed yo' e con o me
my job is not to spend
my job is not to accept yo' paltry pittance
my job is downhome scary
my job is to sirvive
Sir

now listen to my story
                 now listen to me good

my job is pissing on yo' street
my job is sleeping on yo' bench
my job is eatin' yo' scraps like a catfish dog
my job is to wreak my stench
all over prissy park place

oh
      my

  oh
             my

my job traveled overseas
my job went six feet underground
my job walked away like an ungrateful bitch
my job laughs at me on a ticker tape
my job teeters from an eyeful tower
my job trickles from yo' penthouse suite

do you like me now
do you like it

my job is counting crow
my job is to reckon the lies on yo' spineless back
my job sucks yo' blueshit blood
my job rages through yo' deepest fears

now let me entertain you

my job is electric barbwire
my job is to riot through yo' prison
my job is NOT to sizzle on yo' doo dah chair
my job is to rap-rap-a-tat-tat
on yo' whitewashed door
my job is to look you from a glass eye
and shout

doo
     dah

Sacrafishylamb

u r the sacrafishylamb
on the all-
tar of
Kapitoil
izm

youworkyourassoff
2 mayke
         ands
meat

u mount deadt
like a whorse
-thuh car
-thuh mort
gage
-thuh credebt crd

yr jb iz krncht
withalltheother
numb
ers

sum daze we +d
sum daze -tract

its awl 4 the
   e
  co
  no
  me

1 day
son
yule apre

sheate
all that weave
dun fr
yu

mean
wile
      goahead
      flip them burghers
      french those fries
      re-tail yrself
      fir the hollowdays

izn'it a onederful lief ¿

Shoptalk

The time has come to talk.
There's a riot from 9 to 5
the buildings are looting the street.

Can't you think of something else?
the birds are dying to sing.
Take the subway
see for yourself
the music is deafening
the sky is a distant place.

What do you mean it's come to this?
Yes, I understand
the sharks are on the beach
go to Bermuda
it's safe there
I understand.
There are toothpicks in the forest
you can't find the wind
I understand.
Business is business
you want strawberries for dessert
I understand.
It's part of the plan
I understand.
I understand.

Stop signing those checks and
listen to the lilacs bloom
listen to the rush hour
listen listen
listen to time die.
Yes, I know.
Yes. Yes.
I understand.

Notice III

(Black)

People
who do not conform
to our rigorous standards
need not apply.

Flag Burning

who says
I can't burn your flag

I am the anti-Christ
I am the Moslem terrorist
waiting to shoot down
your twisted idea of democracy
I am the welfare child
sucking on the withered teats of your craven civilization
I am the feeble elder
whose sweat-earned pension
you say drains the nation's budget
I am the drug-scarred ghetto boy
the black-skinned whore
the mambo motherfucker
you would kick out
despite the fact
that I raise your children
scrub your dishes
and mop up the shit you perpetrate day after day

just watch
as I strike the match

and when I rap
you tremble in your spit-shined shoes
when I speak out
you spin your disclaimer machine
when I fight back
you unfurl your cunning laws
hunt for ways to strap me down
proclaiming
you have been sent by the grace of God
you are the savior of all that is good
of all that is sanctimonious
of all that would harm my unworthy, wretched self

listen
as the flag bravely curls up
then cowers
to the crackling flames

and you would safeguard me
by denying me my rights
you would protect me
by filling the streets with guns
you would jail me
for being poor/black/brown
for refusing to play your game
pray your religion
give up the pittance you dole out
in the name of God and the People

the people?

as if IBM personifies the people!
as if Enron represents the people!
as if the NRA
the Heritage Foundation
the Kallous Khristian Koalition
kares about the people!

and you say I can't burn your flag?

here's my reply to your two-tongued promises
here's my response to your soft, serpent lies
here's my answer to the threats you propagate
in the Name of GOD and the PEOPLE

I will be the proud anti-Christ
I will be the Moslem terrorist
I will set your flag aflame
right here at the gates of your White House barn

behold

as the raging flames consume
the banner of your hypocrisy

oanly in am-   erica

oanly in am-
    erica

lief
as
nvr
b4
scene

               dth
               in
               lvng
               klr

real'ty
s   t   r   e   t   c   h   e   d
        a cross
        yr
        screem

               destruktion
re   kon   struk tion

fiktion wreckreate
               d
beefor yr ays

br
  ought
2u
buy
thuh
      reap
          up
              likens

&
theyre
kroners

ownly inn a Merck
                        ah
a
   plaus

a
   plaus

Hitler Is Not Dead
    for Steve Biko

Hitler is not dead
he's swimming in the harbors
of Nicaragua
Hitler is not dead
he's building settlements
on the West Bank
Hitler is not dead
he's razing villages
in El Salvador and Afghanistan
Hitler is not dead
Hitler is not dead
Hitler is not dead
he's in New York
shooting youths on the subway
Hitler is not dead
he's preaching a creed
in a church in northern Idaho
Hitler is not dead
he runs a tenement
in South Central L.A.
Hitler is not dead
Hitler is not dead
Hitler is not dead
he's on channels 2, 4, and 7
rambling on about
heart transplants
and homeless transplants
and homelands in South Africa
Hitler is not dead
he's beneath the gloss
of Time magazine
Hitler is not dead

he's located on your F.M. dial
Hitler is not dead
Hitler is not dead
Hitler is not dead
his seed is in
Nestle's formula
Hitler is not dead
he banks on
B of A
Hitler is not dead
he's the head of
the U.S. Olympic team
Hitler is not dead
Hitler is not dead
Hitler is not dead
he rides the tongues
of Evangelicals
Hitler is not dead
he's a missionary
in Ethiopia
Hitler is not dead
he's a member of
the Peace Corps
Hitler is not dead
Hitler is not dead
Hitler is not dead
he's alive and well and living in Mexico
he's alive and well and living in Chile
he's alive and well and living in Poland
he's alive and well and living in Iran
he's alive and well and living in Israel
he's alive and well and living in Hollywood
he's alive and well and living in your heart
Oh no no no
Hitler is not dead

Bridge

This world is a bridge:
you can see it on TV.

Europe and Asia are connected by a bridge.

They're building a tunnel
between England and France.

A tunnel is not a bridge.

Once upon a time, a woman sat at the piano.

Music is the art of ordering sound.
A musical passage linking two sections of song is a bridge.

Beethoven used gunshots in the Wellington Victory Overture.

A gun is a bridge between life and death.

The warring parties in Bosnia
came to an agreement today.

A son, a husband, a father died in the ceasefire.

A ceasefire is not a bridge.

Later
in a snowy interlude
dodging snipers
and the snap of ice under her untrained boots
she would gather water for her child.

Water is an obstacle between two land masses.

Water goes under a bridge.

During the Gulf War
the Allies destroyed the bridges over Baghdad.

Sometimes a bridge is an obstacle.

Diplomacy is a bridge.

Afterwards
they escorted the refugees across the border to safety.

A refugee is one who escapes danger or persecution.

When the Moslems and Croats were released
after the rape and torture
the survivors searched frantically for food and haven.

Truth is an obstacle that must be conquered.

Childless
the bitter taste of Chopin lingering on her fingertips
she begged for mercy at the border.

A border is not always a bridge.

Across the sky,
someone paints a masterful scene.

TV is a bridge between truth and fiction.

History is a secret that somehow survives.

Conquer the world with truth.

Weather Report

It will be mostly unstable today
with chemical clouds blanketing the sky.
During the early hours of the morning,
clouds will clear up
leading to a mix of Apache helicopters
and Tomahawk missiles.
Artillery shells will fall through the day
and there will be scattered skirmishes
throughout the metropolitan area.
Diplomats and unembedded journalists are urged to take cover.

Falling statues are expected to threaten most of the country today
and there is a high likelihood of anarchy
leading to a loss of law and order
and five thousand years of history.

The national weather service has issued
a depleted uranium warning for most of the region.
Today's predicted accumulated fallout:
several thousand acres of life and limb.

Extended forecast:
Roads leading to Syria and Iran
are expected to be choked
with tanks and advancing troops.
A travel advisory has been issued
for civilians in and beyond those areas.

Tonight's forecast:
clear skies and
bombs over Baghdad.

Today's weather

courtesy of
the
Uknighted Stakes of Amerika
& its affiliate Ltd.

Collateral Damage

(we regret the loss of)
    civilian casualties
(we regret the loss)
    of innocent bystanders
(we regret the)
    loss of independent observers
    the loss of unembedded reporters

(we regret)

(we regret the)
    Ministry of Finance
(we regret the)
    Press Building
(we regret)
(we regret)
    the Ministry of Culture
    Children's Hospital
    the pharmaceutical facility
(we)

(regret)
(regret)
(regret)

(the loss of)
    doctors
(the loss of)
(the loss of)
(we)
    nurses
(we)
(regret)
(the loss)
(of)

        medical supplies
(the lossof)
        syringes
        pain killers

(the lossof regret we)

(regret)
        history
(the loss of)
(we apologize)
(we're sorry for your)
        geographical location
        your house
        your museum
        your market
(we regret the)
(regret)
        the bridge across the river
(our condolences for)
(our deepest sorrow)
(our commiseration)
(our pity for)
        your baby
        your wife
        your son
        your husband

(we regret the)
(thethethethethethethethe)

(we regret the)
        values
(we insist)
(we claim)
(we maintain)
(we regret the)

       liberation
(we)
(loss the regret of)
       occupation
       oil
(we regret)
       the country
(we maintain the regret of)

(we regret the loss of)
       freedom
(we regret the)
       constitution
(we regret the lossof)
(we regret the lossof)
       freedom of press
(we do)
(we do)
(we do so regret)
       freedom of speech
(the lossof the lossof the lossof)
(the)
       right to a fair trial
(thethethethethethethethe)
       right to counsel
(we regret the)
(we)
(we)
(we)
(we regret)
(we so regret)
(we do so regret)
(we do hereby declare)
(we swear on our mothers)
(we swear on the flag)

(we swear on the bible)
(we swear on the corporation)
(we're sorry)
(the number you have)
(we're really sorry)
(we sincerely apologize)
(we can't express our)
(we regret the loss of)

War of the Month Club

January   Gulf War
February   The Apache Wars
March   War on Iraq
April   Spanish-American War
May   Mexican-American War
June   Korean War
July   World War I
August   Vietnam War
September   The Balkans
October   The October War
November   Battle of Guadalcanal
December   World War II

Two Soldiers

I read
with anger
today:
the death of two soldiers.

Mutilated.
Throats slit.

Two mothers' angels.
Two fathers perhaps.
Two men
two lovers
their women
as yet
unaware.

The Pentagon denied
the allegations:

there is no evidence
there are no indications

the men were pummeled with stones.

A medical examination
they said
contradicted witness
and military reports.

To the wife
the child
the lover
to the mother
sitting by the fireside
looping a ribbon

to fasten to her front porch
death is death.
Murder is murder
and war
no matter how portrayed
is still unhappily war.

There are no accounts
that buffer the pain.
There are no excuses
no political expediencies
that restore
what has been so senselessly lost.

there is no evidence
there are no indications

And yet
from the day you savaged Iraq
from the day we lifted our voices
in mighty opposition
from the day the Iraqi soldiers
were killed
mutilated
pummeled by weapons of mass destruction
we have heard
nothing
but
excuses
political expediencies

and with our voices raised we said

there is no evidence
there are no indications

And we were treated like traitors.
We were dismissed:
uninformed citizens
exercising their democratic rights
while the Iraqi mother
the Iraqi child
the Iraqi lover
awaited the dreaded news
that would never come.

Where is the justice in this quagmire?
Where are the weapons
where the open arms
we were promised
you would find?

there is no evidence
there are no indications

So we say to you
with voices still strong
we proclaim
to all who will listen to our clamorous cries
who will hear our shameless words
who will see
what they do not wish to see

there is no evidence
there are no indications

And the time has come
to bring
our brothers and sisters
home

You Really Don't Love Me

You really don't love me
it's in your eyes
you really don't love me
it's in your lips
you really don't love me
it's in your hands
you really
you really
you really don't love me
it's in your breast
you really don't love me
it's in your perfume
you really don't love me
it's in your IUD
you really
you really don't
you really don't love me
it's in your soup
you really don't love me
it's in your dollars
you really don't love me
it's in your processed food
you really
you really don't love
you really don't love me
it's in your schools
you really don't love me
it's in your TV
you really don't love me
it's in your magazines
you really
you really don't love me

Notice IV

People
of all
                                                            (Christian)
faiths
are welcome.

Raw Footage

--after Leonard Cohen

I was sitting watching the news
and there were bombings and killings and all the usual kinds of violence
being perpetrated against innocent people in all parts of the world
and they were talking about this 16 year old Palestinian boy
who had strapped explosives around his waist
so that he could blow up some Israeli guards at the border crossing
and I was wondering what could make someone so young so desperate.
Then they told us how the kids had all made fun of him
because he was short
how he was promised 23 dollars and 7 virgins if he blew himself up.
Then they brought his mother and she was crying and complaining
about the people who take advantage of children
the most vulnerable of the vulnerable in this sick sad world
and I asked myself how a people could become so hopeless
that they had so little left in this life, that they had given up everything
that the last and only thing they had to offer was the only way
they could imagine that there was even a glimmer of hope that they would get out of
this situation that had kept them prisoners for so many years

I was reading a book about the holocaust
and there was pain and suffering and pathos beyond the
capacity of human endurance
and I remembered a time when I was a child of 6 or 7 years old

I was at a friend's house and there was a movie playing on the TV
and I watched as a roomful of women holding babies and young children were herded naked into showers
and when the spigots were turned on there was gas instead of water
and I watched in horror as the women held on tight to their children
in their one last gasp of motherly love
and the pain was so great that I closed my eyes and wished that I hadn't been there in that room at that time but the image by then was so seared into my memory
that even today as I write these words, as I wonder how much misery
could be caused in name of politics and power
the pain is still so great that I consider ending my life
just to stop it, just to ease it just a little bit
because so many people have suffered, so many people are still suffering at the hands of the greedy
for reasons that even the wildest animals could not comprehend

I was walking down Constitution Avenue
in this capital of the free world
where the archives of democracy are housed in a museum not far from here
where the president of this great country resides in this not so great era of our history
and I came upon a man huddled by a fire wrapped in an oily, grimy cloth
and I looked beyond the feigned smile and the request for spare change
I looked into his vacant eyes and his hollow face and I saw raw fear
draped over his frail frame like a pall
the face of a man who was enduring the last indignity

in a long line of indignities his people had faced when they
    were wrested from their villages
when they were shackled and sold and beaten and stripped of
    every ounce of humanity
and I looked into his eyes and I saw myself
and I thought this could be me lying in the street hungry and
    cold
this could be my son, my daughter, my wife, my mother, my
friend
it could be you my friend
it could be anyone of you, lying out there helpless and
    destitute
wondering what angry god could have allowed any and all of
    this to happen

I was sitting at my desk writing a poem
or a story or some other piece of nonsense
that some venerable publication might see fit to print between
    its pristine covers
and I was thinking that maybe I could make a difference
that maybe *we* could make a difference
that maybe we could do something about the pain
other than write poems or sing songs or paint pictures
or talk about it over cocktails or huffed over a hot mug of
    Starbucks
or hiding behind our newspapers in our cozy cafes
while the homeless and the destitute parade outside
like ghosts, invisible in their veils of pain
because it could be you my friend, yes you
or the person sitting beside you or the person sitting across
    the room
take a look now, stand up, walk around, try to feel your
    neighbor's pain
because we are all in this together my friends
because my friends as we share this moment now
we are all getting closer to that time when we will eventually
    be in pain

whether we become destitute or homeless or maybe lose a
   spouse or a loved one or maybe you'll wake up one morning
   and find yourself alone looking in the mirror
asking yourself what have I done with my life, wondering
   where all the friends are
as you pick up the razor blade and wonder whether you
   should use as directed
or to make one simple cut across the flat of your wrist instead
and I want you to promise me my friends, that when you leave
   here tonight
while you're going home by yourself or with your loved one or
with your friend
and you come upon someone who is in pain
maybe one of the homeless that live just behind this building
or the woman who has been abused by her husband
or the teenager who's selling his body on the street corner
   because he ran away from home and doesn't know any
   other way to survive
or the man who is recklessly shooting his gun because he lost
   his job, or his wife or his best friend to some
   incomprehensible act of violence
or the street whore who hides her wretchedness behind a
   patina of heavy makeup
when you see any of these people I hope that you will go
   beyond your shrugged shoulder or your offer of spare
   change or your attempts to assuage your guilt
that you will do something bigger and braver to help ease the
   pain of your brothers and sisters
and if you promise me this tonight my friends, then maybe,
   just maybe, for just once
in these long, miserable, painful 52 years --
I might get just one complete night of rest.

After the Beheading

What they did
they did
in the name of god

in the name of god
as long
as I have
head
or tongue
or hand
I will not remain silent

in the name of god
not spit nor brass
shall glorify them

no god
shall pull asunder
what god has rendered

no man
shall render god
in what they do

for god
in his magic
will render godless
all their godliness
for magic
in godly wisdom
will render holy
on this horrid, bloodless day

on this day
no god

shall remain
holier than thou

on this day
there will be
no god

but god

in the name of god
I do hereby swear

We of Greenwich Village Cafe Days

We of Greenwich Village cafe days
      cold-water bohemian lofts
         sidewalk, sideshow art displays
We of poetry/Ginsberg/Ferlinghetti
      and other coney islands of the mind
We of Jack Kerouac
      Ken Kesey
      Merry Prankster hipster talk
We of Marx/Lenin/Mao Tse-Tung
      Baez/Dylan/the Beatles
      and all cultural revolutions
We of alternative music
      alternative lifestyles
      the Village Voice
      the Free Press
We of Mary Jane smoke rings
      electric kool-aide acid trips
      phantasmagoric magical mystery tours
We of flower power
      free love
We of anti-war
      anti-imperialism
      anti-anti-anti and
      give peace a chance man
      bring our brothers home
We of Lennon/Ono love-ins/happenings
      long-haired-iconoclastic-up-against-the-wall-dude
      -and-hey-man-ya-dig-like-we-got-to-love-one-another
      -right-now-cause-we're-hip-ya-see-like-we-got-to-make
      -the-world-a-better-place philosophications
We of Maharishi meditations
      Hare Krishna, Krishna Krishna
      the Zen, the Zodiac, the Dalai Lama
      Castaneda-mescal-minded landscapes

We of ideas and ideals
    fine books/fine art/fine wine
We of relevant education
    strikes
    demonstrations
    sit-ins and teach-ins
We of women's lib
  of feminist aspirations
We the children of Kennedy
    of King
    of Chavez
    who dared to make waves
    who challenged McCarthy and brought Nixon to his
    Krazy Krooked Knees
    who promised the world the dawning of the Age of
    Aquarius and barely survived the Eve of Destruction
We who inherited the holocaust
    the bomb
    the Berlin Wall
  who tried to escape the flames of the Cold War
        the images of melted steel
            melted flesh
      brains splattered before our living-room eyes
We who witnessed the race of Good against Evil
      the conquering of the moon
      the victory of science
  who proclaimed that God was dead
  wrote the obituary for hope
  serenaded the mistress of despair
We who marched through the streets
    carried the cross that others would burn
    manned the picket lines
    fought the battles
      the police
      the water canons

        the rubber bullets
        the appropriators of the modern state
We who remained patriots
        stood fast by the constitution
        demanded the rights we were taught were ours
   and were greeted by dogs and batons
    who stood by as the self-proclaimed guardians of democracy
                                    freedom
                                      and liberty for all
            mocked those same self-evident truths
            commissioned the re-creation of hero worship--
                                  Superman
                                  Rambo
                                  the Force
                                  the Reagan
                                  phenomenon
            and institutionalized the Age of Greed
                                  AIDS
                                  Development
and we watched silently
     dropped a coin in a tin cup
     took our usual seat in our frosted, darkened cafe window
     sipped our Perrier
          our decaffeinated cappuccino
     tsk-tsked/lamented
     turned another page of the New York Times
                        the Wall Street Journal
                        the Washington Post
as the nation threw its citizens out on the streets

We of Greenwich Village cafe days
   who never dreamed it could be this way
We watched silently
   turned another page

We of Greenwich Village cafe days

Paper Cranes
(for Anthony)

Paper cranes
yellow, red
orange origami
child-made cranes
strung like trawls of fish
in Nagasaki and Hiroshima

some fall off and
drift like autumn leaves
shrouding the countryside
like flames weeping
tumbling like autumn leaves

some fall off and
drop like tears
mourning the charred earth
like wailing widows
raining like silver tears

some fall off and
whisk away in the wind
speckling the dazed sun
like ashen memories
howling in the fiery wind

some fall off and
glide gracefully to the ground
thin, delicate
paper cranes
like snowflakes
falling to the ground

some fall off and
spread like cherry blossoms

pinken the brown earth
like gossamer on the horizon
papering the world with cherry blossoms

some fall off and
sail up to the sky
rising on blue wings
like dandelion dreams
floating up to the sky

some fall off and
make it back to America
scattering over the cities
like confetti
like multi-colored messages

paper peace cranes
swarming over America.

Conquer the world with peace.

About the Author

Mike Maggio has published fiction, poetry, travel and reviews in *Potomac Review*, *Pleiades*, Apalachee *Quarterly*, *The L.A. Weekly*, *The Washington CityPaper*, VOL. *NO MAGAZINE*, *Gypsy*, *Pig Iron, DC Poets Against the War*, of which he is an active member, and many others. He is the author of *Your Secret is Safe With Me* (Black Bear Publications, 1988), an audio collection of poetry, *Oranges From Palestine* (Mardi Gras Press, 1996), a chapbook of poetry, and, most recently, *Sifting Through the Madness* (Xlibris, 2001), a collection of short fiction. His work has been met with critical acclaim, with the Midwest Book Review recommending his short story collection as "a grippingly written, sometimes frightening, but always deeply involving anthology." He is currently working on a new collection of concrete, visual and collage poetry entitled *Once Upon a Blank Page.* He lives in northern Virginia with his wife and three children.